TABLE DECORATIONS

TABLE DECORATIONS

JANET BRIDGE

a Salamander book

Published by Salamander Books Limited
LONDON

Published by Salamander Books Ltd.
129-137 York Way
London N7 9LG
United Kingdom

© Salamander Books Ltd, 1995

Distributed by Random House Value Publishing, Inc.
40 Engelhard Avenue
Avenel
New Jersey 07001

A CIP catalog record for this book is available
from the Library of Congress.

ISBN 0-517-14171-X

CREDITS

Managing Editor: Joanna Smith
Photographer: Simon Butcher
Stylist: Janet Bridge
Art Editor: Paul Johnson
Americanized by: Constance Novis
Color Separation: P&W Graphics Pte Ltd, Singapore
Printed in Singapore

CONTENTS

Introduction

INTRODUCTION

Appliqué tablemats are simple to make and can be used many times to create different effects with other decorations on the table.

As the cost of eating in restaurants increases and home cooking becomes more adventurous, entertaining at home has become an enjoyable pastime for many people. Arranging your home to welcome your guests is part of the preparation; the warmth of the welcome and the atmosphere you have created adds to the enjoyment of the occasion. The amount of money you spend is immaterial. It is the presentation that really counts. If you have spent some time and effort your guests will appreciate the thought you have put in and enjoy themselves from the moment they step through the door. Obviously the meal itself is important but so too is creating a visually pleasing setting and the right atmosphere whether at a formal dinner party or a relaxed supper with a few friends.

Fresh flowers have always been a popular way of dressing a table and are suitable for any occasion. When you make an arrangement, though, do take into consideration the amount of space available. Only too often, pretty centerpieces have to be moved to make space for serving dishes. Also, the height has to be taken into consideration. There is nothing more frustrating than not being able to see your fellow diners across the table and it makes conversation very difficult. The obvious way to get over this difficulty is to keep a flower arrangement low, but another option is to stand it on a pedestal. I have included an arrangement on a pedestal cakestand (see page 12) to show you how to do this. Alternatively, instead of having one large arrangement in the center of the table, why not have a series of smaller arrangements around the table?

When choosing flowers for an arrangement, there are many factors to consider. You may wish to select colors to match your crockery or the decor in your dining room or even complement the food you are serving. The occasion may also be a consideration. For instance, you may wish to set the scene with red roses for a romantic dinner for two, but it would be better to choose lots of pretty white flowers for a family gathering. Whatever the occasion, look around the garden or in the florist's shop to see what is available and remember to avoid poisonous plants.

Candlelit Meals

There is nothing quite like the warm, soft glow of a candle and rarely can it be created any other way. The soft pools of light create an intimate atmosphere which is very flattering to the faces around the table. There are numerous types of candle available in all colors, shapes, and sizes. Alter candles are ever popular, while floating candles are a relatively new idea and are now available in a range of different designs and colors. When combined with a few fresh flower heads, they make an effective floating arrangement for the center of the table; choose the flowers to complement the occasion. Outdoor candles are also now readily available and are perfect for warm summer evenings. If any wax spills on the tablecloth, scrape off the excess with a knife then cover the mark with brown paper or kitchen towel and press with a warm iron. Remove any remaining color with methylated spirit but check the cloth for colorfastness first.

Below: This elegant centerpiece will scent the room with a soft, flowery fragrance and will go on giving pleasure well after the meal.

Above: The tradition of presenting gifts at the table is a long and happy one. These spice tins are one of the many gift ideas in this book.

Choosing Crockery

If the crockery you purchase is going to be used every day, then it is advisable not to spend too much money and to check whether it is dishwasherproof, if necessary. The choice is endless and there are so many styles and patterns now available that it ultimately comes down to personal preference. However, I have found that a plainer design is more versatile, because it can be dressed up to create whatever style you like. The addition of a checked tablecloth and cotton napkins tied with gingham ribbon, for instance, makes a homey, country style, while using the same china on a bold tablecloth with brightly-striped napkins can create a thoroughly contemporary feel.

Remember that with careful thought and planning you can create a setting for any occasion whether it is inside or out, summer or winter, formal or informal. I hope the ideas in this book will help you to do this and inspire you to devise schemes of your own.

Below: These dainty fabric bags are a lovely way of presenting mints or other candies to your guests to eat after the meal.

Right: A simple posy of wheat ears and dried flowers on each side plate lifts a plain table into a pretty, thoughtful scheme.

CHAPTER ONE

CENTERPIECES

A centerpiece is a must for every table, whether
it is at a formal dinner or a buffet. Creating a focal point will help add
balance to the scheme. Any of the ideas in this section will certainly provide
the first topic for conversation among your guests.

Christmas Cone Basket

1 Cut the foliage into short lengths and strip the ends to create a stem on each. Wrap a wire around the base of each cone, twist the ends together and leave one end long. Lightly spray a few of the cones with gold paint.

2 Wire three plastic oasis holders onto the base of the basket and push a thoroughly soaked oasis onto them. Insert a thick layer of foliage around the oasis to create a good base for the arrangement. Push two candles into the oasis.

3 Add cones and more of the foliage to the arrangement, working your way from the base to the top, making sure the oasis is well covered. Add gold cherubs, wired ribbon bows and twigs as finishing touches if you have them.

Harvest Roses

1 Glue two oasis holders to the base of the basket and push a block of dry oasis on top to fit snugly into the basket. Spread glue around the rim of the basket and press dry sphagnum moss onto it. Trim off any long ends.

2 Trim the dried wheat, leaving 2in (5cm) of stem on each ear. Working from the basket handle to the edges, insert the wheat stems into the foam close together so the foam is not visible, leaving a narrow margin around the sides.

3 Trim the stems of some dried roses to a similar length and insert into the oasis around the edges of the basket, with their heads resting on the rim. Use tweezers to hold the stems to prevent damaging them.

Cakestand Centerpiece

1 You need a soaked oasis ring which fits on your cakestand. Start by cutting the conifer foliage into short lengths and strip the ends of the stems. Insert around the outside edge of the ring and repeat in the center with shorter pieces.

2 When the foliage ring is complete, cut the stems of the flowers and the other types of foliage to the right length. Build up the flower ring, adding extra foliage between them to create softness. Aim to achieve a good balance of color.

3 Place the ring on the cakestand and make any necessary adjustments. Add a few stems of trailing ivy and some extra flowers hanging down below the rim of the stand to make a graceful cascade around all sides.

Terracotta Candlepots

1 Line the base of a small terracotta flowerpot with dry oasis foam. Stand the candle on the foam and check it is at the right height. Cut further pieces of oasis to fit around the candle and hold it securely in place.

2 Start to add the dried flowers around the candle. Begin with a thick ring of deep pink, dyed flowers. Leave the stems quite long so they will stand up above the outer flowers and remain visible around the candle.

3 Next add florets of dried pink hydrangea, filling up the space and allowing the outer flowers to hang down over the edge of the pot. Finish with a few dried nigella seedheads at intervals to add extra interest.

Citrus Ring

1 Snip off some evenly-sized laurel leaves and insert them around the edges of a soaked oasis ring. Repeat with some smaller leaves around the inside edge of the ring.

2 Attach wires to a selection of fruits so they can be inserted into the ring. Insert wires through the bases of the large fruits and twist the long ends together, but make wire staples for the smaller fruits and push them right through.

3 Build up the arrangement by adding the large fruits first and adding the smaller ones between them. Add extra leaves to fill any gaps. The fruit must not be eaten from this centerpiece, it is purely decorative.

Spring Garden

1 Take a shallow terracotta bowl and line the base with gravel to increase drainage. Next fill the bowl with potting soil and firm lightly. Choose a few pots of spring plants such as primroses, snowdrops, dwarf daffodils, and ivies.

2 Remove the plants from their pots and gently set into the soil, arranging them evenly around the bowl to give a balanced appearance. Firm the soil around them and add more if necessary. Water lightly.

3 Cover the surface of the soil with moss. Terracotta is porous, so you will need to stand a mat under the bowl to protect your table. If you wish to keep the plants after the meal, take them out of the bowl and repot them as they were before.

Buffet Table Display

1 Wrap three elastic bands around a tall galvanized bucket 4in (10cm) from the top rim. Repeat with another three 4in (10cm) from the bottom rim.

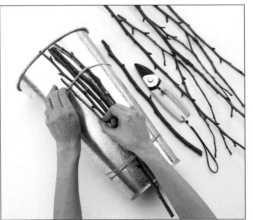

2 Trim down a number of straight twigs and slip them under the elastic bands. Arrange them close together and continue around the bucket until the outside is covered.

3 Use two thick bundles of raffia to tie around the bucket and cover the elastic bands. Use short pieces to tie the raffia bundles to the elastic bands. Fill the bucket with sunflowers.

Dried Legume Plate

1 Draw around your dish onto a sheet of tracing paper, then draw a pattern on the paper. Using the pattern as a guide, paint each area of the plate in turn with glue and stick the larger beans to it in neat rows using your fingers.

2 Stick a line of large beans around the areas that you are going to fill with smaller legumes such as couscous or small lentils. Paint the area with glue and then pour the legumes on top. Press then shake off the ones that haven't stuck.

3 A star outlined in black peppercorns makes a strong centerpiece for the design. We filled in all the space around it with yellow split peas to set it off. When the design is complete and the glue is dry, give the dish three coats of varnish.

Miniature Garden

1 Stick some plastic oasis holders onto a large plate using a strong adhesive. When the glue is dry, push pieces of dry oasis foam onto the spikes leaving a margin of about 2in (5cm) around the edge of the plate.

2 Cover the top and the sides of the foam with dried bun moss, pushing the pieces close together so there are no gaps between them. Hold the pieces of moss in place with pieces of florist's wire which have been bent into staples.

3 Choose a selection of different dried flowers and trim the stems down. Insert the flower stems into the moss, arranging groups of the same flower to give a natural look. Arrange other flowers between the clumps of moss.

Pasta Bow Vase

1 Spray the dried pasta bows with two coats of adhesive varnish to seal them.

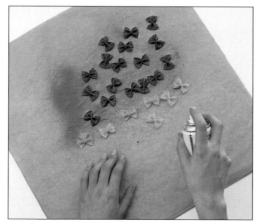

2 Next apply the paint using an aerosol. This method is much quicker and more efficient than using a brush. Paint the bows in a number of different colors if required.

3 When the paint is dry, glue the bows to the vase in any pattern you like. We chose a simple row around the neck of the vase.

Gilded Fruit Basket

1 Using a glue gun, stick together a selection of different nuts to make small clusters. Once the glue is dry, lightly spray the nuts with gold paint using an aerosol.

2 Next spray a selection of artificial fruits with the gold paint, aiming for just a light covering to allow the colors of the fruits to show through. Lay some of the fruit in the basket to create a firm base, gluing it together as you go.

3 Continue to add the fruit and the clusters of nuts until the arrangement is complete. As a finishing touch, lightly spray a stem of artificial ivy and wind among the fruit.

Scented Bowl

1 Wire together a small posy of dried lavender, dried miniature roses and dried gypsophila, creating separate layers of color. Repeat to make four posies in all and trim the stems of each.

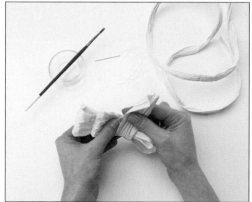

2 To make the bows, take a piece of paper ribbon and fold both ends into the center to make two loops; sew or stick into place. Repeat with a shorter length and attach on top. Make the knot by wrapping a short piece around the center.

3 Stick a mound of florist's putty on each end of the bowl and push two bundles of dried flowers into them, with the stems facing each other. Once the putty has dried, use a strong adhesive to stick a bow at each end to cover it.

Jeweled Vases

1 Using an extra strong adhesive, glue colored glass nuggets onto the outside of a clear glass vase. You may have to do one side at a time and allow the glue to dry before you start on the other side.

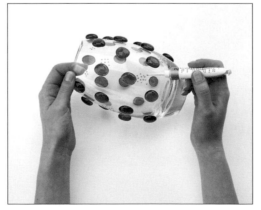

2 Decorate the spaces between the nuggets with spots of gold glass paint and leave until completely dry.

3 Choose flowers which will complement the color and style of the vase, such as these bold tulips and bright daffodils.

Fruit Bags

1 Cut out four burlap rectangles 4x10in (10x25cm) and six 8x12in (20x30cm). Fold each in half, right sides facing, and machine- or handstitch up both sides to create ten little burlap bags.

2 Turn the bags through, taking care to push the corners out square. Fold the tops of the bags over and roll to about halfway down the sides.

3 Fill the bags with a selection of different fruits that your guests can enjoy after the meal, either as a dessert or with their coffee. Arrange the bags on a tray or in an open basket.

Ice Salad Bowl

1 Take two bowls, one 3in (8cm) smaller in diameter than the other. Place the small bowl inside the large one and fill the gap between them with water. Stand a heavy weight in the small bowl and tape across the top to hold in place.

2 Place the bowls in the freezer, and when the water starts to turn to ice, remove from the freezer and slide slices of fruit and sprigs of herbs and foliage into the iced water, pushing them well down between the bowls. Return to the freezer.

3 When the water has frozen completely, take out of the freezer and remove the weight and adhesive tape. Stand the bowls into a basin of cold water and pour more water into the small bowl; the two will eventually come apart.

Cellophane Bouquet

1 Strip the lower leaves from the flowers and foliage. Take 10 to 15 stems and tie tightly together in a bunch. Then add the other stems around the central bunch, at a slight angle to make a neat spiral. Tie and trim the stems level.

2 Lay the bouquet on a large sheet of cellophane and bring the sides up over the flowers. Stick the edges together with adhesive tape, then gather the cellophane tightly around the stems and tie in place. Trim the cellophane level with the stems.

3 Lay two squares of cellophane, one on top of the other. Place the stems in the center and bring all the edges up around the flowers. Gather around the stems and tie tightly. Pour water between the flowers to fill up the "bag" at the base.

Floating Flower Heads

1 Wrap a large elastic band around a shallow glass bowl. Trim the stems from some large ivy leaves and slip the leaves under the band, making a neat row right around the bowl.

2 Tie a narrow ribbon around the bowl to cover the elastic band and finish in a bow. Fill the bowl with water.

3 Snip the heads off some flowers and float them in the bowl. We have chosen white chrysanthemums and asters, but roses will also look very effective. Add a few floating candles and light them just before the meal.

Sunflower Wreath

1 Take a handful of hay and lay it on a flat 10in (25cm) wire ring. Wire in place and repeat until the ring is covered. Tie pieces of raffia around the ring at intervals to cover the wire and hold the hay close to the ring to form a neat circle.

2 Make four small posies using some strands of hay, ears of wheat, artificial sunflowers and a few dried flowers. The posies should have flat backs and a similar arrangement of materials in each. Hold the stems together with wire.

3 Tie the posies to the hay base with raffia and finish with a bow. Space them equally around the ring, all facing the same way. This would make a lovely centerpiece for a summer lunch, indoors or out.

Miniature Rose Basket

1 Wrap some long trails of ivy around the rim of the basket and hold them in place with wire which can be threaded backward and forward through the wicker in a stitching action. Line the basket with polythene.

2 Half fill the basket with potting soil, remove the roses from their pots and arrange on the soil. Add more soil to fill the gaps between the rootballs of the plants and firm lightly around them.

3 Water the soil until just moist, then cover the surface with moss until the soil is no longer visible. If you wish to keep the roses after the meal, take them out of the basket and repot into their original containers.

CHAPTER TWO

TABLECLOTHS & MATS

Tablecloths and mats form the basis of the scheme upon which you can
build the other elements. Once you have made the cloths and mats in this section
you can use them time and again, perhaps combining them with different
centerpieces, napkins, or crockery for a range of different effects.

Plaid Table Setting

1 Cut two pieces of green fabric and one piece of thin wadding 17x14in (43x35cm). On the front of one piece of the fabric, arrange two pieces of plaid ribbon so they form a cross in one corner and sew in place. Sew matching piping along both edges of both pieces of ribbon.

2 Next cover a ³⁄₄in (2cm) button with green fabric. Cut an 8in (20cm) length of ribbon and sew the ends together. Sew small running stitches right around one edge of the ribbon and pull tight to gather up. Oversew to secure. Sew the button and tassel in the center of the rosette.

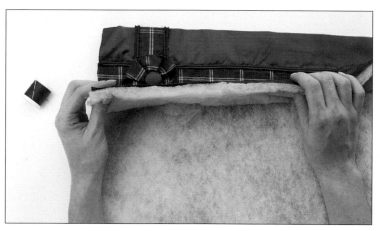

3 Sew the rosette onto the fabric where the ribbons cross. Arrange the two pieces of fabric right sides together and lay the wadding on top. Sew the three layers together right around the edges, leaving a small opening. Turn through and press. Slipstitch the opening.

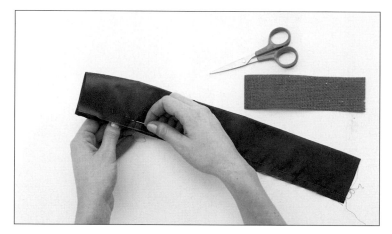

4 To make the napkin ring, cut a piece of stiffening 2x8in (5x20cm). Next cut a piece of the green fabric 5x16in (13x40cm) and fold in half, right sides together, down the length. Sew the long edges together, turn through and press.

5 Slide the fabric tube onto the piece of stiffening, gathering it up as you go. Bring the ends of the stiffening around together and overlap by ¹⁄₂in (1cm); sew in place. Fold under the raw ends of the fabric and sew together. Adjust the fabric to make the gathering even.

6 Make a rosette as before, but cut down the width of the ribbon by ¹⁄₂in (1cm) before you start, to make the rosette smaller. Attach a button and tassel in the same way and sew onto the napkin ring.

Appliqué Mat

1 Draw a flower design on a sheet of paper and cut out the elements to make templates. Iron an adhesive backing onto some fabric remnants, then pin the templates onto them. Cut out the flower, stem, and leaf shapes.

2 Cut out a piece of fabric 7in (18cm) square. Arrange the flower pieces on it, remove the backing paper and iron them in place. Sew around the edges of all the pieces using blanket stitch for a decorative effect.

3 Fold a ½in (1cm) seam around all sides of the square of fabric and press to hold. Position the fabric in the center of the tablemat and pin, then sew, into place. Finish by adding a cross of red thread at each corner.

Fresh Flower Garlands

1 These garlands hang gracefully around the sides of a table; you can position the flowers at the corners of a square table or loop them evenly around the edges of a circular table. Tie thread around the muslin where you want them to be.

2 Make up a series of similar bouquets using a range of fresh flowers chosen to suit the occasion. Remember that the flowers will only be visible from one side and they will be hanging upside down. Wire the stems together.

3 Wire the bouquets to the muslin where you have marked with thread. Cover the wires with a large ribbon bow. Attach the muslin swags to the tablecloth by using safety pins or by sewing on behind each bouquet.

Gold Star Scheme

1 Draw three different-sized stars on paper and cut out. Cut a potato in half and pin a paper star on the cut surface. Cut around the star with a craft knife then cut away the excess potato, leaving the star sticking up in the center. Place face down on kitchen paper and repeat with the other stars.

2 Using a small paintbrush, apply a generous amount of gold fabric paint onto a potato star and make a print on a white tablecloth. Apply more paint to the potato and print another star on top of the first, turning the potato slightly to get a 10-sided star. Repeat with stars of different sizes.

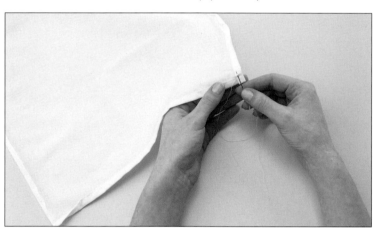

3 When the cloth is covered with a random pattern of different-sized stars, make a set of napkins to match. Cut out 18in (45cm) squares of white fabric and hem all the raw edges. Either print the napkins with a random pattern of gold stars as before or just print one star in the center.

4 To make a napkin ring, cut a length of gold cord about 16in (40cm) long. Bind both ends of the gold cord tightly with gold thread to prevent them from fraying.

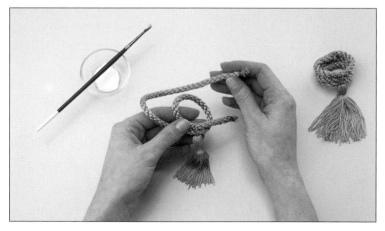

5 Take a gold tassel and thread the cord through the loop at the top. Take the end of the cord around in a circle and thread through the loop again. Repeat until you have three neat circles of gold cord threaded through the tassel loop. Tuck the ends in at the back and glue to the inside of the ring.

6 Lay the table and position the crockery and centerpiece. When everything is in place, sprinkle the center of the table with gold glitter to add a sparkle to the scheme.

Gingham Setting

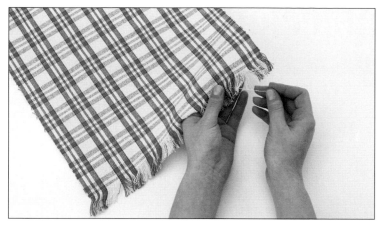

1 Cut a rectangle of gingham fabric 16x12in (40x30cm) for each tablemat. Remove some of the threads from each of the short ends to leave a fringe about 1in (2.5cm) deep. Hem the long sides to keep the edges neat.

2 Using red embroidery thread, cross-stitch a simple heart motif in the top left-hand corner of each mat.

3 To make a napkin ring, cut a piece of gingham 14x3in (35x7.5cm). Fray the ends by 1in (2.5cm) as before then fold in half lengthway, right sides facing, and sew the long edges together. Trim the seam, turn through, and press.

4 To make a salt dough heart mix 2 tablespoons of plain flour, 1 tablespoon of salt, 1 teaspoon of vegetable oil and 2 tablespoons of water. Mix the ingredients thoroughly, then knead for about 5 minutes until you reach a smooth, firm consistency.

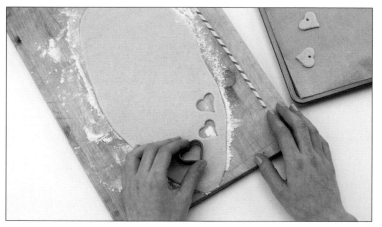

5 Roll out the dough on a floured surface to about ¼in (½cm) thick. Cut out small hearts with a pastry cutter or knife and make a hole in each with the end of a drinking straw. Transfer to a cookie sheet lined with waxed paper and bake in a cool oven for two hours.

6 When the hearts have cooled down, paint with red acrylic paint. Take a gingham napkin ring and tie in a loose knot. Using red embroidery thread, sew a salt dough heart on the knot of the napkin ring to hold it in place, passing the thread through the hole in the heart.

Bluebell Tablecloth

1 Draw a bluebell design on a piece of thin cardboard and cut it out using a sharp craft knife to make a stencil. The design can be as simple or as complicated as you like; you could even trace your design from another picture.

2 Lay your stencil on the tablecloth and draw around it lightly with a pencil to create the flower shape. Repeat at intervals all over the cloth, varying the angle for added interest.

3 Paint the flowers using fabric paints. Again, you can make the painting as simple or as detailed as you wish depending on how experienced a painter you are. Once dry, press the cloth on the reverse side to "set" the paint.

Braid-edged Overcloth

1 Pin the piping cord around the edges of the cloth, easing it neatly around the corners. The edge of the piping tape should meet the edge of the cloth, with the cord on the inside. Stitch in place and oversew the ends of the cord.

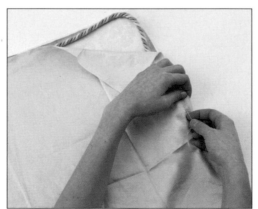

2 Lay the lining fabric on top of the cloth, right sides facing, with the cord between them. Stitch the layers together, keeping close to the outer edge of the cord and leaving a small opening. Turn through and slipstitch the opening.

3 Remove 6in (15cm) lengths of cord from the tape and sew the ends to prevent fraying. Tie into loose knots and sew in place. Thread the loop of a tassel through the middle of each knot and stitch one to each corner of the cloth.

Patchwork Mat

1 Draw a pattern of squares and triangles and color in. Cut out 2in (5cm) paper squares to correspond with your pattern and cut some in half to make the triangles. Cut out a 3in (7.5cm) square or triangle of fabric for each to match your pattern and tack onto the paper templates.

2 Sew the patchwork pieces together along all their edges, following your pattern as a guide to positioning them. Take out the tacking and paper and press. You will be left with raw edges around all sides of the rectangle that the shapes have formed.

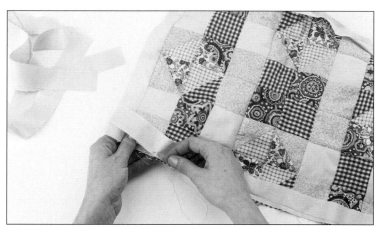

3 To make a border, cut out two strips of fabric 1½in (4cm) wide and the length of the short sides of the patchwork. Sew them to the sides of the patchwork, right sides facing, then turn out and press. Repeat with the long sides, remembering to add the width of the short borders.

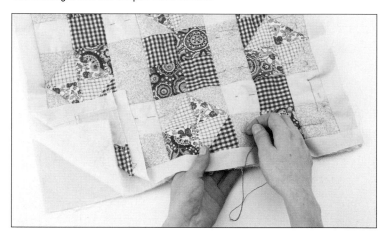

4 Cut a piece of fabric for the back of the mat and a piece of wadding the same size. Slip the wadding between the two pieces of fabric and pin the layers together. Next tack them in place, starting from the center using very large stitches all over the mat.

5 Quilt the triangles in the pattern by sewing small running stitches around all sides, ¼in (½cm) in from the edges through all layers. Remove the tacking stitches.

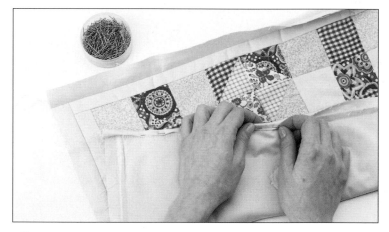

6 Cut four more 1½in (4cm) strips of fabric to form a binding around all sides of the mat. Lay onto the front of the mat, right sides facing, and stitch in place. Fold back and under the mat and stitch to the backing, enclosing all the raw edges. Repeat with the other three sides. Press the mat.

Seashell Mat

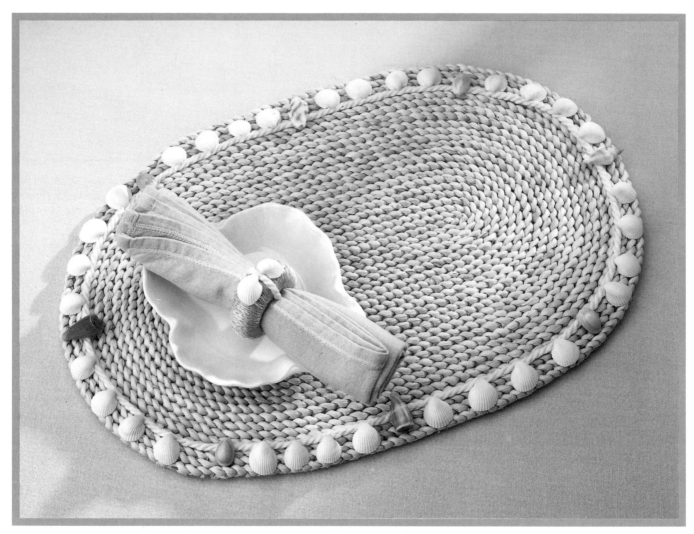

1 Take a length of soft cord and glue it around a plaited raffia tablemat, approximately 1in (2.5cm) from the edge.

2 Lay the shells on the mat with their edges butted up against the cord. It will be easier to arrange the shells evenly if you position the feature shells first, then fill in the gaps with cockle shells. Glue in place with a strong adhesive.

3 To make a matching napkin ring, glue a length of cord around a raffia-covered napkin ring. Place a shell on either side and glue securely in place.

CHAPTER THREE

NAPKINS, GIFTS & PLACECARDS

Thoughtful finishing touches, such as handmade placecards and napkin
rings of your own design can really make the meal a memorable occasion
This section also includes bright ideas for presenting small gifts to
your guests at the table.

Fragrant Fruit Gifts

1 These are lovely, festive, scented gifts that your guests can take home to enjoy. Fill a small terracotta pot with dried oasis foam. Take a florist's spike and place it in the center of the oasis. Secure in place using wire staples.

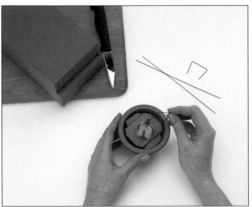

2 Insert a ring of small laurel leaves into the foam all around the florist's spike to cover the foam and hang over the edges of the pot. Tie a piece of raffia around the florist's spike and finish with a bow. Fray the ends of the raffia.

3 Insert cloves into the orange to give it a spicy scent. If the skin is tough, pierce it with a darning needle first. Push the orange onto the florist's spike until it covers about half the spike and the raffia is still visible underneath.

Spice Tins

1 The spices are wrapped individually inside the tin. Cut off the corner of a plastic bag to make a pouch, fill with cloves and tie the top with string. Make a little bag from a fabric remnant, turn the top down and place the cloves inside.

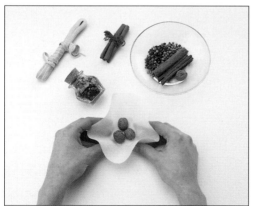

2 Tie a small bundle of cinnamon sticks together with orange raffia, then fill a tiny glass jar with peppercorns. Place three nutmegs in the center of a circle of muslin, bring up the sides then tie the top with fabric tape.

3 Arrange all the spices in the tin and add a few dried bay leaves to add to the decorative effect. Place the lid on the tin and wrap a long piece of fabric tape around the tin a number of times, finishing with a bow. Tuck two bay leaves under it.

Gingham Baskets

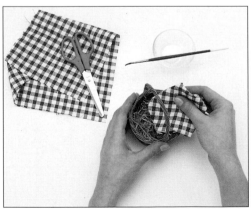

1 Take a small basket and partly fill with shredded wood. Cut a piece of gingham large enough to cover the shredded wood, tuck the edges underneath and push it down inside the basket, then glue in place.

2 Fill a miniature flowerpot with reindeer moss and glue in place. Add a few tiny dried flowers and glue them on top. Tie six ears of wheat together with raffia, trim the ends, and finish with a ribbon bow.

3 Arrange the flowerpot and wheat bundle in the basket. Add a loaf of miniature, artificial bread and a few dried or artificial flowers and glue into place. Your guests will welcome these keepsakes to remind them of the occasion.

Fruit Placecard Holder

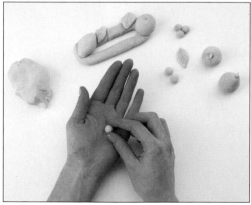

1 To make the salt dough, follow the directions on page 37. First make the base by rolling a sausage shape, bringing the ends together to form an oval and flattening it. Make a selection of fruits and leaves and gently press onto the base.

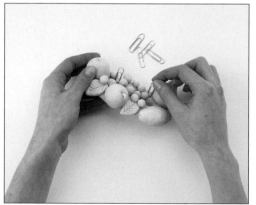

2 When the placecard holder is assembled and you are happy with the arrangement, take two paperclips and press them into the dough at the back of the holder so they stand upright and will hold a namecard.

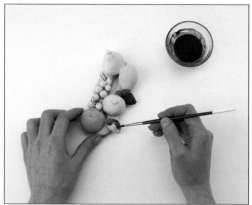

3 Bake the placecard holder in a cool oven for at least two hours until baked through, then leave to cool. Paint the fruits and the base, adding as much detail as you like, then apply a spirit-based varnish to preserve the salt dough.

Pretty Mint Bags

1 Cut a rectangle of sheer fabric 12x6in (30x15cm). Turn one of the long sides over by ¾in (2cm) and press. Turn it over again and tack, then sew, in place.

2 Fold the fabric in half with wrong sides facing. Sew down the side and along the bottom to form a bag. Trim the seam and turn inside out. Sew down the side and along the bottom again to enclose the raw edges inside.

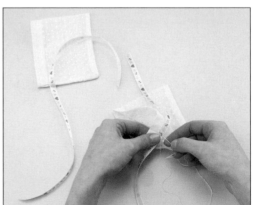

3 Turn the bag through again and press. Sew a length of ribbon to the side seam near the top of the bag. Fill with mints and tie the ribbon in a bow around the top of the bag. The mints can be eaten with coffee after the meal.

Chocolate Boxes

1 Draw a rectangle 2x2½in (5x6cm) on a piece of thin cardboard to form the base of the box. Add a 1½in (3cm) wide rectangle on each side of the base to form the sides of the box. Cut out, score around the base and fold up the sides.

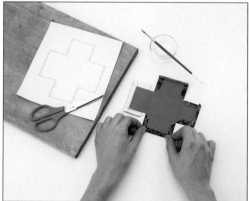

2 Draw around the box on a sheet of patterned paper, adding an extra ½in (1cm) all around. Cut out and glue onto the outside of the box, overlapping the edges inside. Cover the inside with a piece of paper slightly smaller than the box.

3 Fold up the sides of the covered box and punch a hole in each corner. Tie the sides of the box together with ribbon to hold in place. Fill the box with shredded tissue paper and chocolates, for your guests to eat after the meal.

Potpourri Jars

1 Pick the flowers from some stems of dried gypsophila and grind in a mortar and pestle. Repeat with dried pink larkspur and blue delphinium and put to one side.

2 Other flowers can be snipped down to size with scissors. Use this technique with dried marigolds, achillea and mauve statice. Make sure the pieces are small or the petals will not form well-defined layers in the jar.

3 Fill the jar with layers of petals, pressing each layer down firmly with the pestle before you start the next. Add a few drops of an essential oil to enhance the fragrance, then replace the lid. Tie a ribbon around the neck of the jar.

Soap Giftboxes

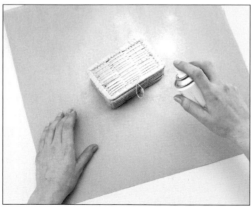

1 Spray a small wicker box lightly with white aerosol paint and allow to dry.

2 Wrap ribbon around the sides and base of the box and secure with adhesive tape. Tie another piece around the lid and finish with a bow on top. Stick a few shells on top of the bow using a strong, clear adhesive.

3 Half fill the box with shredded wood or tissue paper. Add a selection of shells, soaps, and bubblebath sachets with a seaside theme.

Celebration Crackers

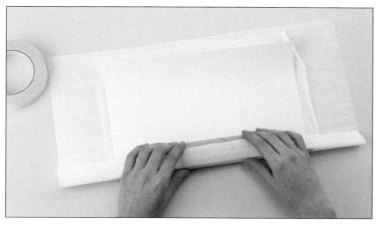

1 Lay a sheet of crêpe paper 10x14in (25x35cm) on a work surface and place a sheet of tissue 10x13in (25x32cm) on top. Place a piece of stiff paper 10x12in (25x30cm) on top of this, then a 4in (10cm) piece of cardboard tube in the center. Roll the layers up together and stick.

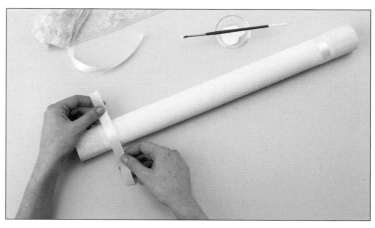

2 Glue some lace around each end of the tube, tucking the loose end just inside the free edge of crêpe paper at the back of the cracker. Glue a ½in (1cm) wide piece of ribbon around the tube about ½in (1cm) in from the piece of lace at each end.

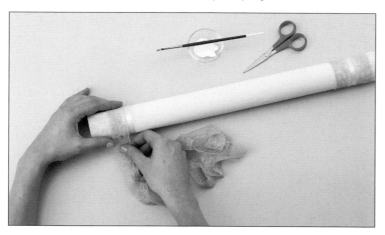

3 Take some narrow lace ribbon with a decorative edge and glue a piece on each side of the ribbon at either end of the tube. Tuck the loose ends inside the edge of the crêpe paper as before.

4 Slip a gift inside the cracker if desired (these crackers are nice enough to be used merely as keepsakes for your guests, so you don't have to add a gift) then gather each end up and tie firmly with nylon cord. Tie a lace bow around each piece of cord to cover.

5 To make the cameo center, iron some adhesive backing onto a small piece of silk. Cut out a cameo shape, remove the backing and iron the silk onto a piece of wide lace ribbon.

6 Glue a piece of fine lace ribbon around the silk to cover the rough edges and embroider an initial or a name on the silk if you wish. Place the cameo in the center of the cracker and lightly glue the lace in place around the cracker.

Fabric Candy Parcels

1 Choose a fabric or selection of fabrics to fit in with your color scheme. Lay a dinner plate on the back of a piece of fabric and draw around it. Cut out the circle with pinking shears.

2 Choose a selection of candies such as chocolates or mints for your guests to eat after the meal. Lay on the fabric and bring the edges up around the candies.

3 Tie the parcels with ribbon or fabric tape to secure the tops. These parcels can be placed on side plates before the meal or just on the table next to each setting.

Miniature Topiaries

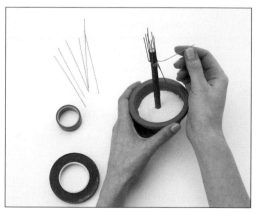

1 Secure the base of a twig in a terracotta pot with plaster of Paris. Take some short pieces of florist's wire and tape them, around their middles, to the top of the twig. Bend up the bottom halves of the wires so they are sticking straight up.

2 Take a small oasis ball and cover with dried moss, holding the pieces in place with staples made from short pieces of wire. When the ball is covered, trim off any loose moss, then press the ball firmly onto the spikes on top of the twig.

3 Insert small sprigs of dried gypsophila and alchemilla all over the surface of the ball to make a soft base. Add a few dried miniature roses and delphinium flowers for color. Finally, cover the surface of the pot with bun moss.

Tissue Paper Rose Bouquets

1 Cut a piece of tissue paper 10x5in (25x12cm). Fold over one third down the length. With the fold away from you, tuck in the top left corner then roll up the tissue paper to make a rose. Tuck in the top corner and twist the stem to finish.

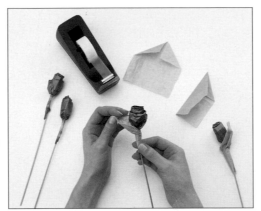

2 Stick a wooden skewer to the stem and cover the join with tissue paper. Repeat with as many roses as required. Make leaves from small squares of tissue. Fold down the top corners, fold in half down the length and attach to the stems.

3 Arrange the roses into a posy and tie the stems together. Lay on a sheet of tissue paper and wrap it around them as you would wrap a bouquet. Wrap a ribbon around the stems and finish with a bow.

Pressed Flower Placecard

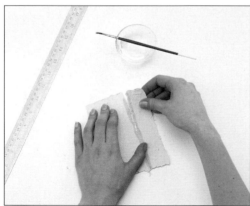

1 Make the placecard from a sheet of handmade paper. To tear handmade paper, mark out the placecard in pencil, then wet the paper along the line using a paintbrush. Leave to soak then carefully tear the paper along the moist line.

2 Fold the card in half and check that it stands up. Arrange pressed flowers on the front of the card along the bottom and up the right-hand side; add a small motif in the top left corner for balance. Choose a single flower for the back.

3 When you are happy with your design, stick the flowers in place using thinned glue applied in dots on the back of each flower with a wooden skewer. Allow the glue to dry, then write the name of the guest in the space provided.

Découpage Placecards

1 Cut out a series of motifs from magazines, greeting cards, or giftwrapping paper. We have chosen cherubs and flowers. Cut a piece of card 4x5in (10x12cm) and spray gold with aerosol paint. Fold in half when dry.

2 Score lightly along the fold with a craft knife. Arrange the cherub and flowers on the card and glue in place, making sure the cherub's head protrudes above the fold in the card.

3 Using a sharp craft knife, cut around the head of the cherub as far as the fold line on both sides. Now fold the card in half and the cherub's head will stand proud of the fold.

Velvet Napkin Ring

1 Cut two rectangles of velvet 3x8in (8x20cm). With right sides facing, sew three sides leaving a short end open; turn through. Sew across the width of the fabric ½in (1cm) from the closed end. Sew from the first seam along the center of the fabric to within 1in (2cm) of the open end.

2 You should now have two long pockets in the fabric. Stuff with lengths of cylindrical foam, pushing the foam in place with the blunt end of a pencil and working until the two sides are even. Sew across the width enclosing the foam, then turn in the raw edges and slipstitch the open end.

3 Using a rivet gun, make three rivet holes in each end of the napkin ring through the unpadded section. Thread cord through the holes and lace up as you would a shoe. Tie the cord in a neat knot or bow and slip a rolled napkin through the ring.

Harvest Posy

1 Arrange some ears of wheat into a neat bunch and add a few dried flowers to complete the posy. Wire the stems together tightly to hold firmly in place.

2 Braid three pieces of raffia, finishing the ends with knots as shown. Leave the loose, unbraided ends long.

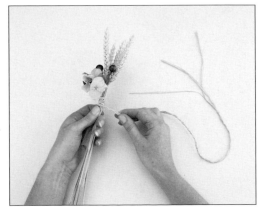

3 Tie one end of the raffia braid to the posy stems. Then wrap the braid around and around the stems to cover the wire. Finish by tying the loose ends of the raffia into a small bow. Trim the stems of the posy.

Christmas Gift Baskets

1 Wrap a piece of narrow plaid ribbon around and around the handle of a small basket and secure each end with adhesive tape or glue. Attach a sprig of artificial hollyberries to the base of the handle on either side.

2 Lightly spray four small pinecones and a few artificial leaves with gold paint. Attach wires to the bases of the cones and use the wires to fix the cones, two on each side, to the basket handle. Attach the artificial leaves in the same way.

3 Finish by tying a ribbon bow at each end of the handle, ensuring all the wires are covered. Fill the baskets with little Christmas gifts or with candies for your guests to eat after the meal.

Tussie Mussies

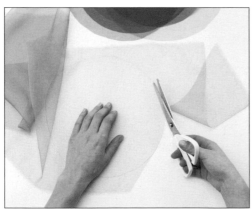

1 Using a dinner plate as a template, cut out four circles of sheer fabric for each tussie mussie, using a mixture of colors or just one color for each.

2 Choose a selection of flowers to complement the fabrics you have picked. Make little bouquets of flowers and foliage and wire the stems together to hold in place. Trim the stems to size, then cover the stems with green florist's tape.

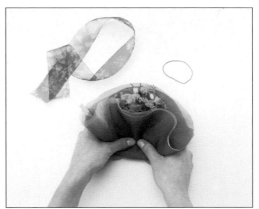

3 Lay four circles of fabric on a work surface and place a posy on top with the ends of the stems in the center of the fabric. Bring the fabric up around the flowers and secure around the stems with an elastic band. Cover with a ribbon.

Valentine Giftbox

1 Cut some long strips of tissue paper and crunch up in your hand. Draw two small hearts on corrugated paper and cut them out. Finally, make three tiny tissue paper roses (see page 56 for instructions).

2 Paint glue all over the top of the box lid. Starting from the outside edges, lay strips of crunched tissue on the glued surface to cover it completely. Stick the paper hearts and roses on top and finish with curled paper ribbon.

3 Allow the glue to dry thoroughly, then spray the outside of the box and the lid with gold paint. Allow the paint to dry. Then fill the box with shredded tissue paper and a gift.

Index